The world works better...

The World Works Better
by Danny Iny

ISBN: 978-0-692-97782-8

How to Use This Book

This isn't one of those books that you have to read in one direction from the start to the end. Feel free to jump in on any page!

Each page finishes a sentence about what makes the world work better, but the end of each sentence is the beginning of a journey…

…because the story isn't inside this book. The story is inside YOU.

So take time to think and talk about each page. What does it mean for you? What does it mean for the world — what would happen if more people followed this idea?

Use this book as a starting-point for conversations with yourself, with your children, or even with your team at work.

And keep it as a reminder that all the adventure, discovery and limitless potential of childhood are yours to enjoy — at any age.

The world
works better...

...when we help each other

...when we share

...when we're always learning

...when we try new things

...when we know
we have choices

...when we tell the truth and keep our promises

...when we tidy up our messes

...when we look for ways to fix problems

...when we believe that fun is important

...when we know hard work can be fun, too

How to Make the World Work Better

It was a bright, sunny autumn day. As I was walking down the street, lost in thought, a blur of motion caught my eye. Just up the road, a mother and her son were riding their bicycles. The mother's tire must have snagged on something, because her bike suddenly flipped over, landing with a crash.

I was one of several neighbors who sprinted to their aid and sat with them until the paramedics arrived 20 minutes later. As the mother was loaded into the ambulance, her son thanked us. These words came unbidden to mind and out of my mouth:

"The World Works Better When We Help Each Other"

I made a mental note to share that sentence with my two-year-old daughter and with others, too. I thought of more and more people with whom I wanted to share these simple words: my family, my friends, my employees, my students, and everyone who follows my work. We all implicitly understand it but, all too often, we forget.

Then the list of things I wanted to share began to grow. After all, the world doesn't just work better when we help each other. It also works better when we share. When we do our best. When we stand up for what's right. And more....

That led to the creation of this book, a reminder to all of us of what we already know about how to make our world work better.

Danny Iny

Founder/CEO at Mirasee
Montreal, Canada

About the Author

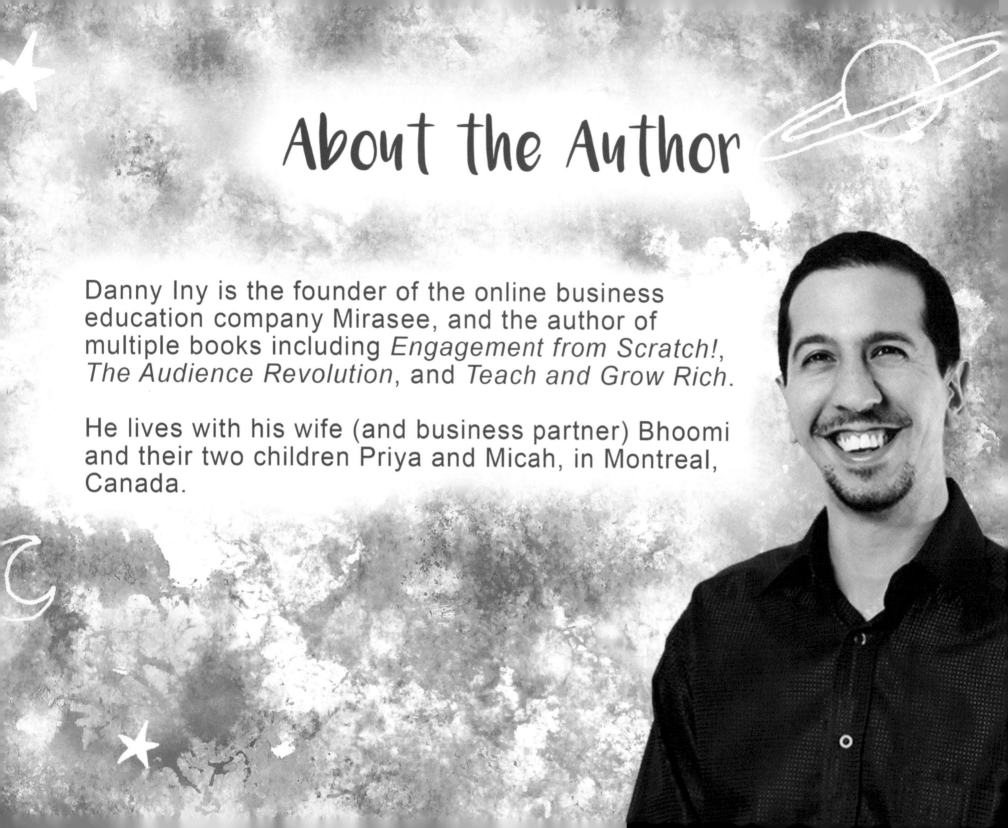

Danny Iny is the founder of the online business education company Mirasee, and the author of multiple books including *Engagement from Scratch!*, *The Audience Revolution*, and *Teach and Grow Rich*.

He lives with his wife (and business partner) Bhoomi and their two children Priya and Micah, in Montreal, Canada.

Acknowledgements

Bringing this book from idea to fruition would not have been possible without the contributions of several people.

Thank you to Luca Mendieta, who created the beautiful illustrations in this book.

Thank you to Sophie Lizard, our content editor who brought my message to life.

Thank you to Ashlee "Tree" Branch, our creative director who oversaw the production of this book.

And thank you to Bhoomi, Priya, and Micah, who inspire me every day to look for ways to help the world work better.

CPSIA information can be obtained
at www.ICGtesting.com
Printed in the USA
BVHW061340240822
645427BV00018B/6

* 9 7 8 0 9 9 9 6 5 0 0 9 7 *